How Did You Get Here?

A Book & Documentary on the paths we take in life and the different end results that may come no matter who we are and where we come from.

Brittany D. Phillips

authorHOUSE®

AuthorHouse™
1663 Liberty Drive
Bloomington, IN 47403
www.authorhouse.com
Phone: 1 (800) 839-8640

Published by AuthorHouse   05/27/2017

ISBN: 978-1-5246-9201-8 (sc)
ISBN: 978-1-5246-9199-8 (hc)
ISBN: 978-1-5246-9200-1 (e)

Library of Congress Control Number: 2017907540

Print information available on the last page.

This book is printed on acid-free paper.

Credits to DTOWN Studios for the Author Photo

A documentary and book about different people from all walks of life and how the different roads they took led them all to a different outcome. No matter what, we all have our own destiny and our own paths to take so the choice is left for you to decide, no one else can do it for you.

Contents

Introduction

This book idea came to me from personal experience. I wanted to show our youth that no matter where you come from, your background, your family and past; you can be and do whatever you set your mind to. The things we want most will not be easy, but they will be the hardest to accomplish, if you really want it you have to fight for it and keep it pushing. I have interviewed people from different cultural backgrounds, areas of the world, and lifestyles that have all accomplished things that they may or may not have planned but that's how life goes

and we can ALL do it! I've included poems that I have written overtime and just want to share to also show that you can express yourself in many different ways. Overall, I hope that everyone can gain something from this book/documentary and share it with the world.

<u>Mrs. Charlotte Fowler-White</u>

Age: 52

Occupation: Retired Army 31 Years

Born and Raised (location(s)): Houston, TX

Educational Background: Bachelors Degree

Where you raised with both parents, one parent, or other; how did this affect you?

I was raised with both parents and I experienced a lot of love.

Did you have siblings, if so, how many?

I had 11 siblings (5 sisters and 6 brothers).

What is your current family situation now, (i.e. single, married, divorced, single parent, etc)?

I am married and getting ready for my first grandchild August 2017.

When did you realize what you wanted to do with your life and what you had to do to get there (age included if possible)?

When I was 17 years old I knew I wanted to join the army but I did not join until I was 20.

What is one of your favorite quotes?

No favorite quote in particular, just live and enjoy life the best way possible.

What is one piece of advice that you would give a young person of today's society?

One piece of advice for youth would be to always follow your first mind, don't get distracted or let anyone change your mind for you.

What is your view on faith and religion(s)?

I believe in God and that if you stay positive and live right you will have a blessed life. My faith has gotten me through a lot in life and has always brought me home safe.

How did your personal life (family, friends, love) take an effect on you as you strived to reach your goals?

My family and friends were very supportive of my goals and me reaching them since I had been in ROTC for 4 years in my youth days.

As a kid what was your dream to be when you grew up?

I wanted to be a Sergeants Major in the Army.

Where do you see yourself in the next 3-5 years from now?

In the next five years I would like to retire a second time and enjoy life and my family.

About the Author:

I was born and raised in Houston, TX in what most would call the hood. This gave me a very different perspective in life and has molded me into the successful woman that I am today. I have a Bachelor's Degree in Business Management, a Master's Degree in Business Administration, and looking forward to gaining my 2nd Master's Degree in Education Counseling. I am currently 25 years old and very happy with what I've gained in life in my time here so far. I have learned a lot, grew a lot, but mostly learned that I am never too old to learn and wisdom comes in all ages, shapes, and sizes. I have a business of my own named, A Brittany D. Phillips Co. LLC which puts together and promotes events as well as seminars and speaking engagements. I started this back when I was an undergrad in college (2013), and I look forward to the next few years when I can proudly say,

celebrating 10 years. I also am planning to start a non-profit organization for youth and adults to have the means to give back, help others, and provide them with the tools needed for success. Where I came from we did not have all these opportunities or they were hidden from us to keep up from gaining on these opportunities and I am going to change that so the children can be and stay the future as we say. My plan is to have an empire that not only helps but inspires.

Understanding

I just can't seem to understand

Why it's so hard for me to be understood

Yea you hear me you got ears

But are you listening to what I'm saying

Sometimes it's like I'm speaking a foreign language

Or even in sign language

To be heard yet misunderstood

To be seen yet blurry vision

Felt yet only a ghost a tingling sensation without a reasonable explanation

It's how I feel

I know it's not intentional but I'm intentionally frustrated from the repetition and the trying to rephrase and the trying to recreate from the agony and pain

The frustration and illusions driving me insane

Not to mention that we are our own worst critic and we let our minds wonder and play tricks on us

So sometimes in the mist of my passionate words I lose focus and confuse myself

I know my intentions and I know what I mean

But how do I translate for you how do I make you see what I see

Hear what I hear

Breathe what I breathe

Understand the simplicity of me

Just want to be loved and cared for, shown and expressed love to feel secure and appreciated but understood never the less...

Or is that just too much to ask

I have come to believe that it is me

When the majority of the popularity are all
in agree

Then I have to know It's me I'm the odd ball
I'm the difference

Just wish someone would try and listen

False Sense

He gave me a false sense of security
turned my fairy tale around and instead
you showed me

Now I lost my v
My voice for you
My heart that spoke the words that I thought
but yet you didn't know I felt for you

If you knew the pain behind these eyes
The things these walls endure in silence
Showing tears that only God knows about

You'd see that the sad part
Is It isn't a fairy tale
My everyday feels like I'm outside of myself
and that this is all a dream

Like I'm a actor in a movie don't know the words to my scene

I'm looking in a mirror and I then see what everyone else see's when they look at me

Makes me want to walk by the waterfall and wish to dive in

Chill under water

Maybe it'll make my problems fade in

Maybe not I guess instead

I'll b resting in a sea of peace and river of thoughts

My mind is still

Not thinking knowing or wanting

My heart is at rest

No pain hurt or sadness

He gave me a false sense of security
Turned my fairytale into reality
But no I'm no longer waiting for you
It's your turn to play out your sanity

Dr. Sandy Murphy

Age: 62

Occupation: Marriage/ Family Therapist

Born and Raised (location(s): Born Shreveport, LA and raised in Houston, TX

Educational Background: PhD in Education

Where you raised with both parents, one parent, or other; how did this affect you?

I was raised with both parents; father was abusive to mother.

Did you have siblings, if so, how many?

I have 11 siblings, 7 sisters and 4 brothers.

What is your current family situation now, (i.e. single, married, divorced, single parent, etc)?

I am a single divorced mother of two adult children (son and daughter) and grandmother of five granddaughters.

What is one of your favorite quotes?

The devil is plain STUPID! "Don't LISTEN to the devil; you have got to BELIEVE in God".

What is one piece of advice that you would give a young person of today's society?

Take time to get to know who you are and be who you believe you can become. Do not try to copycat somebody else or seek to get along with someone to become a part of their group or clique. There is ONLY ONE creation of YOU. You are authentically beautiful and smart. So why not embrace YOU and SHARE your GIFTS with character-worthy relationships.

What is your view on faith and religion(s)?

Believe in God and have a steady faith.

As a kid what was your dream to be when you grew up?

Coming from a large family of 12, I dreamed and day-dreamed a lot! My first most frequent day-dream was to be in my own space, become a Nurse and a great Author

of many books. I did become an Author of over 21 Books and more coming. I tried Nursing, but I did not continue in it. I am now a Counselor/Therapist. I wouldn't change my dream journey if I could. I am grateful to be living some of my dreams now.

Where do you see yourself in the next 3-5 years from now?

My ultimate goal is to have a debt-free Building for my School of Ministry and Mentoring Academy so I can freely offer more outreach to youth and families.

Having a single parent household:

I grew up in a single parent household and as we all know every situation is different and mines was a blessing. My mom was a very strong force and backbone in my life, which I know has built me to be the force I am. She had help from my grandmother and aunt which was also a benefit to my sister and myself, by not having to move a lot and being able to grow up with family. My mom was in the Army for 31 years so although traveling is great for some, not moving for us allowed our goals to be reached and not have to be uprooted on a constant basis. Things may have even been tough for my mom at times but she never let us see it. She was truly great and one of a kind. We may not realize all our parents do when we're young but as we mature and grow we have a better understanding and I am grateful for that.

My Siblings:

I have 3 older siblings. I have a sister on my mother's side and a brother and sister on my father's side from Los Angeles, California. Fortunately, the distance never kept us apart and my mother made sure I knew them and had a relationship no matter how far.

My Current family situation:

Currently, I am engaged to be married as well as preparing for our first child. Excited to have a growing family and continued growth and success for my business, I plan to leave it to my child/children someday for them to continue the family business. I am going into the field of education because I want a better and closer grasp on helping prepare our youth for the future; being an educator and counselor will allow me to do so. Once I complete my third degree in Education Counseling I will go into the field looking forward to helping guide our youth back to a positive and safe place so that they can come to school and focus on getting their education to give themselves a better future and life that they may have initially imagined.

Trying

I'm trying to be the best woman I can be but he's trying so hard not to love me

I don't know what to do stuck between a hard place and a rock

The rock is on top and every time he lies to me it drops

Just a lil' closer

I don't lie or cheat but he looks for a way out constantly

He's even so mean and I just take the verbal abuse

I used to say girls in my position were dumb for staying

But now I understand that's just what happens when you love and give your all to the wrong being

Too a boy not a man

Listening to what everybody else suggest

Wrong thing to do cause they don't know what's best

They don't know me like you do they don't know your love-my truth

They're on the outside looking in and most are single too

Do you ever think maybe they wish to be in your shoes

Have me cooking and cleaning and loving them instead of you

So hate they must throw you said it yourself

All this fighting between us is just one of Gods test

To see if we'll overcome can we make it thru

Team work makes the dream work so what you gone do

Communication is key but

YOU WON'T LISTEN TO ME

I can't do it alone I'm only human baby

A couple that prays together will stay together if you really want it to

Wish my heart wasn't so weak for you then maybe I'd be able to leave you

Maybe instead have the strength to save the relationship from doom

But the way you push and don't want to spend time with me

Sends me dreams of breaking loose

All I want is you to be here and show me that you care

Give me half of what I give you

Just something so my body can bear

The thoughts of us apart is something I refuse to come true

But sometimes jus cause you love someone

Doesn't mean they are meant....or love you too

Gotta go gotta leave......

Next Lifetime

Next lifetime

I guess I'll see you next lifetime

Reminds me of how we spent the last time

Head going crazy spinning out of control

Trying to reach a grip but can't seem to take hold

Next lifetime

Maybe I'll make the right decisions

Not to be influenced by the ignorance

Not to be confused by the fake confidence

Next lifetime

We can get a second chance

Make a remarkable advance to the life that we planned

The dreams that we want

And the hopes to exceed

Next lifetime

Better friends and foes

No love we thought we knew

No acceptance of the low

The standards a tadpole can reach

No standards indeed

Next lifetime

I won't give my all to the wrong person

Friend or lover

Family sister or brother

But give my all to myself

The only one worthy of my wealth

Next lifetime

I'll be me

Nobody else

No one else's expectations

Just me me me

We should always put ourselves first and stop putting others before us who do not do the same. Love comes in many different forms so be aware of which love you are facing and who it is coming from.

Mr. Elliot Moutra

Age: 34

Occupation: Teacher & Entrepreneur

Born and Raised (location(s)): Houston, TX

Educational Background: BBA Finance from University of Houston-Downtown

Where you raised with both parents, one parent, or other; how did this affect you?

I was raised by my paternal grandparents. I would split time on weekends between by Mom and Dads'. My grandparents' raising me, has given me what people term as an "old soul". I believe has given me a level of patience that most people my age probably don't have.

Did you have siblings, if so, how many?

No biological siblings.

What is your current family situation now, (i.e. single, married, divorced, single parent, etc)?

Single.

When did you realize what you wanted to do with your life and what you had to do to get there (age included if possible)?

I realized probably around 18 that I wanted to one day be my own boss. I've made attempts but haven't gotten there yet.

What is one of your favorite quotes?

"You are free when you realize that you are an aspect of God having a human experience", Professor James Small.

What is one piece of advice that you would give a young person of today's society?

Know your history, and not just one viewpoint. Know what both sides have to say. In the information age, ignorance is a choice. Do not live in comfortable ignorance.

What is your view on faith and religion(s)?

I think that the traditional religions are just another system of control. Because we don't have a true sense of what spirituality is and of God, our idea of religion is entrapping

us rather than liberating us. Faith is an unquestioned belief. If you have it in yourself, you can achieve anything you want.

How did your personal life (family, friends, love) take an effect on you as you strived to reach your goals?

Having a father who has supported me in every way I've needed has been invaluable! I had a major failure as an adult and he was there to pick me up and guide me through recovery.

As a kid what was your dream to be when you grew up?

As a kid, I wanted to be an Engineer.

Where do you see yourself in the next 3-5 years from now?

3-5 years from now I plan to be my own boss, having created something that has transformed my neighborhood into a community once again.

When I knew what I wanted to do:

All my life I knew I wanted to help people and be a big influence for others like myself. By high school I knew I wanted to also write books to show there is no age limit on going for your dreams and being successful. Once I started there was no turning back. It became my motto that, "Success Is The Only Option (SITOO)".

Favorite quote:

"Nothing worth having is easy,
or everyone would have it"

Youth advice:

First and foremost, do not try to be in a rush to grow up. You only see the glamorous parts of being free, dressing how you want, and doing what you feel. No one wants to pay attention to the hard parts and the reality. You have bills that come like clockwork and no one cares if you have the money or not. You have hard days and easy days but you just pray the good outweighs the bad. Something is always happening that is out of our control and all you can do is deal with it, try your best to adjust, or fix it. But at the end of the day, that's adult life and that's reality. Friends and loved ones can give advice but they are not you nor are they living your life so you have to make the best decisions for you and your situation. You are the one that has to live with the consequences of the choices you make. Be careful what you wish for and who you deal with because you never know who truly has your best interest at heart.

Education

Education is the true foundation

It doesn't always mean you have to get the highest degree

But it does come with a level of understanding

It's a difference in being ignorant vs. dumb

Being unknown and unwilling to learn

Compared to simply just don't know

Education is the true foundation of life

Who you know is how you get there

But what you know is what keeps you

Knowing that you're never too old to learn

Understanding that you will never stop learning

So many opportunities in this great USA

It's all on your shoulders if you don't take advantage of the plays

You can be a teacher, doctor, a musician, or dancer

Any career is at your grasp if you own it

Education is so vast that they cover many of things

Too easy to achieve just lazy if you refuse to succeed

L.I.F.E.

Living

It

Fulfilled

Everyday

You never know what to expect

What's around the corner or coming up next

Life is full of twist and turns

Like riding on a rollercoaster

You wish you could be the operator of the ride

But that's just plain impossible

Out of our control out of your hands

You have to learn to take the good with the bad

As much as we hate to admit it

It's the bad that helps mold us to who we are

The one that chooses to fail or shoot high for the stars

When you choose to fail its nobody's fault but your own

Just as you choose to succeed its how you've grown

Don't waddle in a pitty party

Just "accept what happens" and lie to yourself

Fight for your life and your outcomes

Use your best to do your best

Your friend, parents, or significant other don't determine your outcomes

It still circles around to you and the things that you've done

Dr. Farhina Imtiaz

Occupation: Gynecologist: (Women's Health)

Born and Raised (location(s): Born in Pakistan and Raised in Atlanta, GA

Educational Background: Medical Degree

Where you raised with both parents, one parent, or other; how did this affect you?

I was raised with both parents; very strong forces in my life.

Did you have siblings, if so, how many?

I am the oldest of 5.

What is your current family situation now, (i.e. single, married, divorced, single parent, etc)?

I am happily married with children.

When did you realize what you wanted to do with your life and what you had to do to get there (age included if possible)?

I've known since I was a child that I wanted to be a doctor.

What is one of your favorite quotes?

There comes a time when one must take a position that is neither safe, nor politic, nor popular, but he must take it because his conscience tells him it is right.... Martin Luther

What is one piece of advice that you would give a young person of today's society?

Stay in school. You need higher education to get ahead in this world.

How did your personal life (family, friends, love) take an effect on you as you strived to reach your goals?

Not sure completely, but overall my parents had a great influence that has made me the woman I am today.

As a kid what was your dream to be when you grew up?

As a kid I wanted to be a doctor and own a Jaguar.

Where do you see yourself in the next 3-5 years from now?

In the next 3-5 years, I see myself doing more volunteer work and continuing my business.

My view on faith and religion:

My faith has gotten me through so much. Life is complicated; it can be hard and at times very easy but it all depends on how you take it and what you make it. I am a firm believer that everything happens for a reason, so I have come to appreciate not only the good but also the bad. The bad usually prepares you for the better and without it at times we wouldn't be where we are or even who we are today. The bad may be hard or very painful but afterwards you realize how much stronger you are from it. So it may not be easy to see or understand while it is happening but eventually you'll understand why you went through what you did and what you learned from it. All you need is a little faith and belief that anything is possible and everything has a lesson. I don't hold to all the technical rules and regulations "people" set I simply believe in God and my relationship with Him.

How did family-friends-etc affect my path in life:

My family and friends were very supportive and have pushed me to go for my goals my entire life. They have always come to my events, bought my books, and supported whatever it was I was doing at the time in any way possible. Rather it was advice, truthful feedback, or other things of that nature, they were there for me. Without their assistance through my book process and journey with my business venture, I may not have gotten where I am today. I'm looking forward to doing much more and having an empire my family and friends can be a part of as well as proud of. Lastly, the relationships I've had over the years with friends and guys have also pushed me down my path and I am truly grateful.

As a kid my dream:

As a child I wanted to be a singer and actress. I always loved to perform but as I got older I got shy and didn't like how some people would judge others. I still enjoy singing for Church and try to use all the talents God blessed me with. I've also found other ways to express myself and help others which made me the entrepreneur I am today. I love to help in any way possible so I am looking forward to having a non-profit organization to benefit our youth but also our adults and give them the tools and confidence to not only go for their goals but to stick with it no matter what. Maybe one day I'll also be able to be in the music industry writing and creating music which is still a passion that boils inside of me.

Mirror, Reflection

What do you see when you look in the mirror

Who do you see when you look in your reflection

Is it what you want to be

Is it who you want to see

Y-O-U is your biggest road block

Y-O-U is the only thing that creates your outcomes

Not your parents, not your friends

Not your girl, or your man

Do you ever ask yourself where will you be in 5 years, 10 years, then 20

There's so much, yes, plenty of options and choices

Decisions for you to make

As you see you, you, you are the only thing in your way

You think you are ready to be "grown"

But it's not as easy as you may believe

Life is full of ups and downs, ins and outs

And bills, bills, bills

So again I ask

What do you see when you look in the mirror

Who do you see when you look in your reflection

Friends

One o'clock, two o'clock, three o'clock, four

How many friends are waiting at the door

Five o'clock, six o'clock, seven o'clock, eight

Where will they be when it's time to hit the gates

It's easier to say versus easier to do

Sometimes they are there and sometimes untrue

Some are just a lesson and some are unique

Time is the best determiner of what shall be

Will they go through the bad with you or let you suffer alone

Will they be there for you in your hardest times or leave when you need them most

Our lives change, develop, and grow

Our lives change on a constant flow

Never know who will be there

Never know who will go

Sometimes the closest ones are practically family

So how do you categorize the rest

What happens when the friendship is put to the test

Just be careful and prepared for who you think was best

Chef Juan Johnson

Occupation: Executive Chef

Born and Raised (location(s): New Orleans, LA

Educational Background: Degree in Economics

What is your current family situation now, (i.e. single, married, divorced, single parent, etc)?

I am married with 2 children (son and daughter).

What is one of your favorite quotes?

When you waste time you murder success.

What is one piece of advice that you would give a young person of today's society?

Don't waste time, make use of every minute that you get. Follow our dreams and follow your passion.

What is your view on faith and religion(s)?

Provides a foundation for our being, and a higher sense of purpose.

How did your personal life (family, friends, love) take an effect on you as you strived to reach your goals?

My family members were always supportive and pushed me to go for my goals and have a successful career.

Where do you see yourself in the next 3-5 years from now?

In the next 3-5 years, I see myself continuing my successful career as a chef; I've overcome some great obstacles and it's only fueled my fire to accomplish more and push my children in the right direction to accomplish their goals as well.

See myself next 3-5 years:

I plan to have a nonprofit and to continue the growth of my business A Brittany D. Phillips Company LLC. Have a successful career, a happy family, and possibly more kids with a successful marriage. I would love to have more business ventures and partner opportunities that can provide jobs and careers for young adults in college and even adults who would like to be successful in their life time. A Wiseman once told me, "It takes a village to raise a child", I believe if the village continues to be leaders and help each other in life, we can all thrive and be successful.

In Conclusion...

I hope that you all have gained some valuable information and it has opened your minds to all the possibilities that await you. We all come from different backgrounds with different views, morals, and values, but at the end of the day we are all human and equal with options to be who we choose to be. No matter your skin tone, your size, or gender, I believe if you want something you just have to want it bad enough to go through whatever obstacles it may take to get there. As I said before, if it was easy everyone would have it but nothing worth having is easy to attain. I look forward to sharing this information with our youth especially, to prepare them for what lies ahead and open their minds to face reality. Life is not all the glitz and glamour you see on TV, its hard and not always fair, truthfully, complaining won't change a thing. The documentary gives you a true

visual so that you can not only read but see the people who are showing you who they are and how they got there, myself included.

Good luck on your success.......

Special Thanks...

First and foremost, I give all Thanks to God who has brought me through more than I ever thought I could make it through. Next my Mom & Stepdad who are my rock and foundation, and my fiancé Reuben who is my love and my all and really supported me throughout this endeavor. My grandparents, Aunts, and uncles who have always supported and encouraged me, as well as my Aunt Betty who has helped with the editing and completions of my project. To all my family and true friends who have also continued to support me and show up when needed Thank you. Dreams are hard and without you this would not be possible.

Printed in the United States
By Bookmasters